Redleaf *Quick* Guide

Behavioral Challenges

IN EARLY CHILDHOOD SETTINGS

Connie Jo Smith, EdD

D1532164

Redleaf Press®
www.redleafpress.org
800-423-8309

This book is dedicated to my mother, Nevolyn C. Smith, for the many times I have behaved in challenging ways. And to Breanne, who made my life richer by providing me with firsthand experience in facing challenging behaviors of children at home.

Published by Redleaf Press
10 Yorkton Court
St. Paul, MN 55117
www.redleafpress.org

First edition 2008
Cover design by Jim Handrigan
Interior typeset and designed by Mayfly Design
Printed in the United States of America

Library of Congress Cataloging-in-Publication Data

Smith, Connie Jo.
    Behavioral challenges in early childhood settings / Connie Jo Smith.
        p. cm.
    ISBN 978-1-933653-61-7 (alk. paper)
    1. Behavior modification. 2. Early childhood education. 3. Classroom management.   I. Title.
LB1060.2.S589 2008
    372.139'3—dc22
                            2008002122

FSC
www.fsc.org
MIX
Paper from
responsible sources
FSC® C011935

Printed on acid-free paper

U16-08

Behavioral Challenges in Early Childhood Settings

Acknowledgments

Thanks to each of these reviewers for their significant contributions to this work.

Dennis Angle, BA
Stepparent/Foster Parent
Bowling Green, Kentucky

Karen Burger Cairone, MEd
Trainer/Special Projects/Writer
Devereux Early Childhood Initiative
Villanova, Pennsylvania

Jill Orthman Hatch, MS
Early Childhood Consultant
Jeremiah, Kentucky

Luis Hernandez, MA
Early Childhood Education Specialist
Miami, Florida

Amy Hood Hooten, EdD
Infant Toddler Specialist
Western Kentucky University
Bowling Green, Kentucky

Linda K. Likins, MA
Executive Director
Devereux Early Childhood Initiative
Villanova, Pennsylvania

Barbara A. Nilsen, EdD
Author, *Week by Week: Documenting the Development of Young Children*
Port Crane, New York

Janie Sailors, RN
Health Specialist
Orlando, Florida

Melissa Werner, PhD
Assistant Professor of Early Childhood Education
Athens State University
Athens, Alabama

J'Lane Zamora, BS
Owner and Pre-K Teacher
Rocking Horse Daycare and Pre-K
Carrizozo, New Mexico

Introduction

Connie Jo Smith

Addressing children's challenging behaviors can be one of the most emotional and difficult activities you face in early childhood settings. We each bring our own beliefs and experiences to every situation, which can make being objective difficult at times. Inappropriate or emotional reactions to children's challenging behaviors can turn a potential learning situation for the children into an unnecessary crisis. Focusing on the children and on how to help them learn the skills they need to be successful, instead of focusing on our own feelings, is easier said than done, but it's important for us to strive toward. Children imitate behavior they see, so we must be able to model self-control and show children how we want them to act in times of conflict or frustration.

Although this Redleaf Quick Guide suggests strategies you can use for handling some of the most common behavioral issues of young children, it does not provide comprehensive recipes for responding to all situations. Children's behavior is complex and results from any number of causes, such as health, physical environment, temperament, experiences, skills, risk factors, and development. Therefore, all adults working with young children should participate in ongoing training about positive guidance for children. Administrators, teachers, drivers, monitors, substitutes, and volunteers can all benefit from learning more about helping children learn social skills and self-regulation.

Many Challenging Behaviors Represent Typical Development

We must remember that our expectations for young children's behavior should be reasonable for their age and developmental level. Often many of the behaviors adults find challenging are actually typical for certain ages and developmental stages. Children are learning vocabulary and how language works, so they do not always have the words to express themselves to adults or one another in socially acceptable ways. We like to think of childhood as a magical, carefree time. But instead it can be frustrating, because children have not yet learned many problem-solving or coping skills.

Children's emotions can be very intense. Children may not be able to control their feelings, so they need outlets for them and support in learning self-control. Although children may have a growing curiosity about others and the desire to have friends, the social skills guiding them toward knowing how to befriend one another are still evolving. Young children are very focused on themselves, seeing things from their singular points of view. They also have a naturally increased need to be independent, which can create disturbances in the routines of a group of children. Typically developing children may at some times exhibit every challenging behavior described in this book as they carve out their identities. It is the frequency and intensity of the children's challenging behaviors that can alert us to the idea that the behaviors may be outside the typical developmental framework, and that additional support may be necessary.

Developmental screenings of children may help to determine whether children have potential developmental delays or other issues that may impact behavior. Some programs offer developmental screenings, with informed parental approval, and others make referrals for screenings. Screenings, however, alert you only to possible issues of concern and should be followed up with more in-depth assessment if scores indicate a need. Even so, information from screenings may help guide action plans to best support children in reaching their potential in all areas of development. Working together, families and teachers can provide the positive guidance and support needed to help young children through challenging times.

Remaining Calm through the Storm

As you use this book to work with children during challenging times, remember to remain calm. Remaining calm is your very best strategy in dealing with challenging behaviors. Don't become upset, raise your voice, or make threats. These techniques do not work and will make everyone involved feel more out of control. If you are calm, you will be better able to problem solve and to model appropriate behavior for children.

Dr. Connie Jo Smith is on the faculty of Western Kentucky University in Bowling Green, Kentucky. As the director of the Barren River Area Development District Child Care Resource and Referral, Dr. Smith provides support for families and early care and education programs. She is a coauthor of Growing, Growing Strong! A Whole Health Curriculum for Young Children *published by Redleaf Press and* Caring for the Children, Caring for Yourself: A Guide to Promoting Social and Emotional Health.

Aggression

Observed Behavior

- Harming others through kicking, hitting, throwing things, pulling hair, or other aggressive actions
- Destroying property through kicking, throwing, stomping, beating, or other aggressive actions

Appropriate Response

The immediate goal is to keep the child from harming herself or others.

HARMING OTHERS

Infants and Toddlers
- When an infant hits or throws, it is not considered aggressive behavior. Redirect the infant by introducing a different toy.
- When a toddler exhibits aggressive behavior, place yourself between the aggressive child and others. At eye level, tell the child in a calm but firm voice to stop the aggressive behavior because it hurts others.
- Examine the victim to see if there is a physical injury. If there is an injury, follow your program procedures.
- Redirect all toddlers to soothing activities.

Preschoolers
- When a preschooler is aggressive toward another child, place yourself between the child who was aggressive and the victim. At her eye level, tell the aggressive child in a calm but firm voice to stop the activity. Suggest that she take some deep breaths to calm down.
- Tell the victim that you are there to help and ask if she is hurt. Examine her to determine if there is physical injury. If there is an injury, follow your program procedures.
- Once any injury is addressed, help the injured child use words to express her own message to the child who was aggressive.
- Assist each child in regaining self-control and engaging in an activity.

DESTRUCTIVE BEHAVIOR

Toddlers
- When a toddler is destructive, slowly approach and at her eye level, tell the child in a calm but firm voice to stop the activity and return the object to you or to its owner. If necessary offer to trade a different object with the child. Thank her when she cooperates. Assist the child in calming down by suggesting deep breathing or by rubbing her back.
- If another child's work or property was damaged, give attention to and show sympathy for the child whose work was harmed. Help all children involved mend or recreate the work, if possible.
- Redirect each child to a soothing activity.

Preschoolers

- When a preschooler is destructive, slowly approach and at her eye level, tell the child in a calm but firm voice to stop the activity and return the object to you or to its owner. If necessary give the child the option of letting go of the object herself or of your removing it. Thank her when she cooperates. Assist the child in calming down by suggesting deep breathing.
- If another child's work or property was damaged, give attention to and show sympathy for the child whose work was harmed.
- Help the child whose work was harmed use words to express her own message to the child who was aggressive.
- When possible, help all children involved mend or recreate what was harmed.
- Redirect each child to a soothing activity when each has regained control.

> **Don't** show aggression toward the child or instruct other children to use physical aggression as protection. Don't tell the victim's family the name of the aggressive child.

 DEVELOPMENTAL CHECK

Infants and Toddlers

- Infants may communicate by throwing objects or striking at people. This is typical behavior and is not aggression.
- Toddlers lack the verbal communication skills to let you know what they need or want and may resort to aggressive acts to communicate.
- Toddlers have very limited social skills and do not understand the concept of sharing resources and space. For example, when there is only one big red truck, and it is the most desirable toy, conflict that could escalate into aggression is likely.
- Toddlers need to be physically active and mentally engaged. If their physical activity is limited for too long, or if they become bored, aggression may result.

Preschoolers

- Preschoolers may have difficulty with a change in routine. Because they express their emotions strongly, the insecurity caused by a changed routine could escalate into aggression.
- Preschoolers are egocentric and see things from their own points of view. Problem solving is therefore limited by the individual ways in which they perceive a situation. This can cause frustration, leading to aggression.
- As preschoolers' independence increases, it may seem reasonable to them that they should be able to get or do what they want, when they want, and how they want. When you limit their choices, the lack of control they feel may cause their frustration to escalate into aggression.

PRESCRIPTION FOR PREVENTION

The best way to prevent children from becoming physically aggressive is to supervise them closely and plan the play space and activities to address their developmental needs.

Observe
- Recognize when children exhibit behaviors that indicate a need they cannot express verbally. Get involved before the behavior escalates into aggression.

Model
- Model cooperation, helpfulness, kindness, and respect by using appropriate ways of verbally expressing your frustration.

Enhance
- Provide multiple copies of popular toys and ensure adequate play space.
- Introduce activities that help children learn about friendly and gentle touching, such as shaking hands, patting, and hugging.
- Include adequate time in the daily schedule for physical activity, such as running, jumping, dancing, and climbing.

Biting

Observed Behavior

- Biting other children, adults, or himself
- Biting objects that could cause harm to himself or damage the object

Appropriate Response

The immediate priority is to keep the child from harming others or being harmed.

Infants and Toddlers
- When an infant bites, tell him calmly and firmly that biting hurts and then redirect him by offering a different toy or by moving him to another play space.
- Comfort the child who was bitten and attend to the injury (if need be) by following your program's procedures. Redirect the child to a soothing activity.
- When a toddler bites, place yourself between him and the victim, and, at his eye level, say in a calm but firm voice, "No biting. It hurts." Have the biter take deep breaths to calm down.
- Tell the child who was bitten that you are there to help, and ask if he is hurt. Examine him to determine if there is a physical injury. If there is an injury, follow your program's procedures.
- Redirect both children to soothing activities.

Preschoolers
- When a preschooler bites someone, place yourself between the biter and his victim. At his eye level, say in a calm but firm voice, "Stop biting." Suggest deep breaths to help the children calm down.
- Tell the child who was bitten that you are there to help, and ask if he is hurt. Examine him to determine if there is a physical injury. If there is an injury, follow your program's procedures.
- After any injury is addressed, help the biting victim use words to express his own message to the biter.
- Redirect each child to a soothing activity when each has regained control.
- Remain physically close, and supervise to reduce the opportunity for more biting.

> **Don't** bite the child back or instruct other children to bite the child back. Don't tell the family of the victim who bit their child.

 DEVELOPMENTAL CHECK

Infants and Toddlers
- Infants may bite to communicate if they become overstimulated, frightened, or tired.
- Older infants and toddlers may bite because they're teething, which causes gum pain.
- Toddlers have strong emotions but lack the verbal communication skills and self-control to let you know with words what they want or need. Biting may be a result of frustration.

Preschoolers
- Young preschoolers may still be teething, but older preschoolers typically have all of their primary teeth.
- Preschoolers are learning new vocabulary and problem-solving strategies but may resort to biting if these strategies are not working for them.
- Vocabulary and self-control skills increase in preschoolers, reducing the frequency of biting.

PRESCRIPTION FOR PREVENTION

The best solution to biting is to supervise children closely and address gum pain, frustration, and other signs of distress early enough to prevent biting.

Observe
- Be aware of children who seem to have gum pain and/or exhibit behaviors that indicate a need or want that they cannot communicate verbally.

Model
- Use appropriate ways of verbally expressing your frustration, and model cooperation, helpfulness, kindness, and respect.

Enhance
- Address teething issues by helping children keep their gums clean. Provide appropriate items for them to chew, such as wet washcloths, frozen snacks, or liquid-free teething rings.
- Provide a daily schedule that allows for child choice, adequate rest, and comforting activities.
- Provide multiple copies of popular toys, and ensure adequate play space to reduce frustration.

Crying and Whining

Observed Behavior

- Crying or whining with apparent need, pain, distress, or fear
- Crying or whining without apparent pain, distress, or fear but with an inability to engage in activities

Appropriate Response

The immediate goal is to identify and address any physical need or injury. Any short- and long-term emotional issues should also be identified and addressed.

Infants and Toddlers
- Go to the infant immediately, identify and address any physical needs, such as hunger, a wet diaper, or other conditions that might make the infant cry.
- Comfort the infant who may be lonely, fearful, or bored. Hold, gently rock, sing, coo, and give plenty of attention to the infant. Do not worry about spoiling babies.
- Go to the toddler immediately to identify any physical need, physical pain, or emotional issues.
- Address the physical pain of the toddler according to your program's procedures.
- Acknowledge the emotional distress the toddler may be feeling. Offer comfort and reassurance while modeling language to express feelings.
- After she is calm, redirect the toddler to a fun activity.

Preschoolers
- Go to the child immediately to identify any physical need, pain, or emotional issues.
- Address any physical pain according to your program's procedures.
- Acknowledge any emotional distress the child may be feeling and invite her to talk about it. Comfort and reassure the child.
- If the child is crying or whining without apparent physical or emotional reasons, redirect her to an activity she enjoys.
- If the child is crying or whining without apparent physical or emotional reasons, cannot be redirected, and is disturbing other children, locate a place for her to continue crying under supervision, away from the children she was disturbing.

> **Don't** tell the child to stop crying or whining, that they have no reason to cry or whine, or that only babies cry and whine. Never shake a baby or strike a child.

 DEVELOPMENTAL CHECK

Infants and Toddlers
- Healthy infants cry! They cry to communicate all of their needs.
- Infants may cry on and off for a few hours each day during the first weeks of life.
- Older infants and toddlers may begin experiencing separation anxiety at about six months. The intensity, longevity, and regularity of separation anxiety are unique to each child.

- Toddlers can use a few words and phrases to communicate but lack the vocabulary to express their distress in words.
- Toddlers have and show intense feelings.

Preschoolers
- Younger preschoolers may experience separation anxiety.
- Preschoolers rely on crying less than infants and toddlers do, but still resort to it and whining in times of distress.
- Children who are asked to speak and understand languages other than their home language may have more difficulty expressing themselves.
- Preschoolers continue to develop and use language in more complex ways, yet may lack the social skills to always use language appropriately.
- Preschoolers are curious and imaginative, which can sometimes lead to fears that adults may consider unreasonable. These fears, however, are very real to preschoolers.

PRₓESCRIPTION FOR PREVENTION

The best solution to crying and whining is to identify the issues triggering the behavior and address them calmly. Children may sense an adult's tension, which can cause their crying or whining to escalate, so get help or take a break if you cannot remain calm. Try to make children feel welcome and engaged.

Observe
- Look for the behaviors children demonstrate immediately prior to crying so you can use prevention techniques, such as reassurance or redirection.

Model
- Use language to express feelings and practice techniques for building friendships and cooperation.

Enhance
- Build positive relationships with each child, and create an environment where children feel like they belong by saying their names, labeling their personal spaces, allowing them to bring objects from home, and displaying pictures of their families.
- Ensure that you have adequate, consistent, and qualified staffing to address the immediate needs of children.
- Introduce stories and activities that are related to any stressful issues the children may be facing, such as the arrival of new siblings, divorce, weddings, or illnesses.

Defiance

Observed Behavior

- Saying "no" when asked or instructed by an adult to perform an act or stop engagement in an activity
- Refusing to cooperate or ignoring instructions from an adult to begin or stop engagement in an activity

Appropriate Response

The immediate priority is to keep the child from being harmed or harming others. Unless harm is an issue, the behavior, while frustrating to you, may not be critical.

Infants and Toddlers
- Although it may feel like an infant is being defiant, you are feeling only their natural intensity. Meet the infant's needs and develop stress-relief skills for yourself.
- Go to the toddler and, at his eye level, tell him in an enticing voice what you would like him to do next. Be sure to make it sound fun.
- If he says "no," ignore the comment, because his saying it does not necessarily mean he isn't going to follow your direction.
- Show the toddler an object related to the next activity or offer your hand to guide him to the activity area.
- Provide support with statements like, "Do you want me to help you?" or, "Let's go together."

Preschoolers
- Go to the preschooler and, at his eye level, say his name. Using a pleasant tone and positive language, let him know what you would like him to do next. For example, instead of saying, "Stop playing with that truck," say, "It's time to put the truck back on the shelf and go outside."
- Offer choices when possible. For example, offer the child the opportunity to do the task independently or with others, before or after getting his coat on, or "slow like a turtle or fast like a bunny."
- If the child seems unhappy with the direction, acknowledge his feelings. Say something like, "I know you really like to play with that truck, but it is time to go outside."
- If the child continues to be uncooperative and safety is not an issue, let him know that you will check back in a minute to see if he is ready then. Try again shortly.

> **Don't** engage in a power struggle by raising your voice, threatening, or arguing with the child. Don't try to physically force the child to do what you want.

 DEVELOPMENTAL CHECK

Infants and Toddlers
- Infants respond to their immediate needs. Defiance is not the issue.
- Toddlers are becoming more independent and expressive.

- Toddlers say "no" frequently, even when they do not mean it.
- Toddlers lack the verbal communication skills to let you know politely that they do not want to do something.
- Toddlers are rooted in the present moment. Change can be difficult.

Preschoolers
- Preschoolers are becoming more independent and expressive.
- Preschoolers are learning new vocabulary and problem-solving strategies for pleading their cases.
- Preschoolers are egocentric and see only their way of looking at things.
- Preschoolers sometimes become deeply engaged in an activity, and it can take a while for them to let it go.

PRESCRIPTION FOR PREVENTION

The best solution to defiant behavior is to avoid power struggles with children. Building positive relationships with children may go a long way toward positive interaction. Carefully evaluate situations and determine if what you are directing children to do is necessary. Prior to transitions, prepare all children.

Observe
- Notice which children are thoroughly engaged in an activity and may have difficulty transitioning. Let these children know individually about upcoming changes before they happen.

Model
- Use appropriate ways of verbally expressing your frustration. Model respect, kindness, cooperation, helpfulness, and teamwork.

Enhance
- Provide a daily schedule in picture form. Children can see what comes next, and individually prepare children who have difficulty with transitions.
- Plan a daily schedule that is flexible enough to allow for each child's individual rhythm, pace, and choices.
- Include activities that teach respect, kindness, cooperation, helpfulness, and teamwork.

Disengagement

Observed Behavior

- Rarely engaging in meaningful play alone or with other children
- Becoming discouraged and giving up easily when a task becomes challenging
- Easily distracted

Appropriate Response

The goal is to help children feel successful by becoming involved with and finishing a simple task appropriate to their age and stage of development.

Infants and Toddlers
- Based on the infant's age, play with her by introducing new toys and games to help her enjoy being involved and playful.
- Offer the toddler cause-and-effect toys that respond—with lights, sounds, or movement, for example—when she plays with them.
- Use words like "done" and "finished" to introduce the child to the concept of completing a task. Say things like, "You finished your apple," or "You did it."
- Provide suggestions, encouragement, and help so that toddlers learn to finish small tasks in a step-by-step manner.
- Provide toddlers with opportunities for exploration play, such as with dumping blocks.

Preschoolers
- Go to the preschooler who is not engaged and offer two choices that are both acceptable and that will be of interest to her. Say something like, "Tonya, would you like to build with blocks or play the colors game?" Go with the child to help her get started and ease away with an encouraging word.
- Go to the preschooler who has abandoned an activity prematurely and give an unobtrusive suggestion like, "Maybe the piece will fit over here. How about you try that?"
- Go to the preschooler who continues to leave a task unfinished and help her identify small steps that will allow her to finish.
- Go to the preschooler who seems discouraged. Sincerely acknowledge her feelings and then ask some problem-solving questions like, "I wonder what would happen if you tried putting the smaller block on top?"

> **Don't** use rewards, such as stickers, when a child engages or finishes a task. Don't give vague directions like, "Finish up." Don't do the task for the child if she is capable of succeeding with encouragement.

Infants and Toddlers

- Infants learn to engage and become playful when appropriate visual and auditory stimulation is provided, and may not engage when stimulation is lacking.
- Toddlers have short attention spans and are not likely to stay with any activity for long periods.
- Toddlers have a growing need to be independent and may not be able to judge their own abilities in advance, resulting in possible frustration.

Preschoolers

- Healthy preschoolers are curious about their surroundings and may become excitable and, therefore, easily distracted.
- Preschoolers are becoming more independent and expressive about what they want to do or do not want to do. If choices are not of interest, they may not engage.
- Preschoolers have longer attention spans than toddlers, but do not typically remain engaged for long periods of time.
- Preschoolers are learning problem-solving skills but have not mastered them, so frustration may still occur when they are unable to be successful.

PRESCRIPTION FOR PREVENTION

The best solution to lack of engagement is to build the child's confidence and skills by working step-by-step to accomplish one small activity at a time.

Observe

- Observe to see when children have trouble engaging or when their frustration seems to build so that you can intervene and support their involvement and success.

Model

- Model being engaged in activities and having fun, and celebrate openly when there is success.

Enhance

- Provide some activities that have an ending and are self-correcting, such as puzzles and lotto games, to help children understand the concept of "finish."
- Provide open-ended toys, such as blocks, creative art supplies, and dramatic play props, that children can play with for an extended period. Encourage them to explore and try new things.
- Include stories in the daily curriculum that are related to children trying new things, working until a job is done, and feeling proud.

Escaping

Observed Behavior

- Leaving, unattended by an authorized adult
- Hiding from adult view or playing out of sight when the group leaves an area

Appropriate Response

The immediate priority is to bring the child back into the safety of your supervision and to attend to any injury or emotional crisis, while at the same time maintaining the safety of the other children.

LEAVING THE PREMISES

Infants and Toddlers
- Infants cannot leave without assistance. Ask authorized adults to sign infants in and out of the program to add a measure of safety and security.
- Ask to see identification and check pickup permission records when any unknown adult attempts to remove an infant or toddler.
- If a toddler leaves the designated play area, move toward him rapidly, calling his name and asking him to stop and wait for you. It is critical that you not sound angry, which may urge him to move more quickly away from you and into danger.
- When you are close enough, bend down, open your arms, and ask the toddler to come to you, or reach out your hand to him in order to keep him in your care. Ask if he can tell you or show you where he was going.
- Address the need, such as having to go to the bathroom, if it is identified, and let the toddler know he should always stay with an adult.

Preschoolers
- Ask to see identification and check pickup permission records when any unknown adult attempts to remove a preschooler.
- If a preschooler leaves the designated play area, move toward him rapidly, calling him by name and asking him to stop and wait for you. It is critical that you not sound angry, which may urge him to move more quickly away from you and into danger.
- If he does not respond or return to you, say that you want to show him a toy or to play ball with him—something you think will stop and redirect him.
- Once the child is near you, hold his hand, touch his shoulder, or use some other method of contact so you can gently but physically ensure he will remain safely in your care.
- Address the child's need (wanting a coat or having to go to the bathroom, for instance) if one was identified. Tell the child that he should stay with an adult and not open the door or gate unless an adult says it is okay. Follow through if you told the child you had a toy to show him or a game to play.

MISSING

Toddlers and Preschoolers
- If a child is missing from the group, ensure that all other children are supervised and then quickly return to the site where the missing child was last seen. While calling his name in a friendly tone, look closely in, behind, and under all furniture or equipment. Check the child's favorite places (the gym, or the playground).
- If the child is not found quickly, contact program authorities, parents or guardians, and the police for assistance.
- After the child is found, address any physical injuries or emotional issues. Remember that the child may not have purposefully separated from the group and may be frightened. Inform others working with you that the child has been found.

> **Don't** panic, chase a running child, scream, or leave a group of children unsupervised.

 DEVELOPMENTAL CHECK

Toddlers
- Toddlers are learning independence. They typically think they can do much more on their own than they actually can, so going someplace alone when they want to makes perfect sense to them.
- Toddlers may lack the verbal communication skills to tell you what they want. Using their feet to walk somewhere can be a way of communicating their desires or needs.
- Toddlers have only recently learned to run and may feel great delight in practicing this new skill.
- Toddlers are playful and may see hiding from adults as lots of fun—their idea of an innocent game of hide-and-seek.
- Toddlers imitate adults. If adults are going in and out of the room or area without telling others, toddlers may see nothing wrong with doing the same.

Preschoolers
- Preschoolers have a short but growing attention span and are naturally curious. If play opportunities are not interesting to them, they may seek stimulation elsewhere.
- Preschoolers may flee or hide from perceived fearful situations, such as seeing an insect, a loud noise, or another child.
- Preschoolers are taller, stronger, and have greater fine-motor skills, allowing them to more easily and quickly manipulate doors and gates.
- Preschoolers may be shy or just need time away from the group and may retreat to a private space where they do not see or hear the group leaving one space for another.
- Preschoolers may hide from other children or adults to be playful.

PR_XESCRIPTION FOR PREVENTION

A child may hide or escape when there is a lack of close adult supervision. If you can learn more through close observation about why a child escapes or hides, you may be better able to prevent it in the future. Ensuring adequate staffing and close supervision and adding door chimes or secure gate latches can also help.

Observe
- Observe closely to see if children exhibit behaviors that indicate they may have a need that they are not expressing to you verbally. Follow up to meet needs when they are discovered.

Model
- Prior to leaving the group space, inform the other adults of where you are going. Doing so models desirable behavior for children and encourages communication and collaboration between adults.

Enhance
- Position an adult to always have clear view of the exit routes so a child cannot slip out unnoticed. Ensure that doors, gates, and other possible exit routes are securely closed and will create a loud but pleasant sound, such as from chimes or bells, when opened.
- Count all of the children when you enter a new space, such as the playground, and count heads again prior to leaving it. Count the children once more when you arrive at your next destination.
- Keep a sign-in-and-out sheet with you at all times to clearly identify which children are in your care and which ones have been picked up by parents, guardians, or other authorized adults.

Hyperactivity

Observed Behavior

- Moving frequently from place to place or running indoors
- Moving body parts, such as shaking a leg or fidgeting hands, even when sitting or standing in one place
- Frequently looking around, appearing to lack focus

Appropriate Response

The immediate goal is to help children use energy appropriately, learn to relax, and engage in meaningful activities to prevent boredom, high levels of frustration, and accidents.

Infants and Toddlers
- Introduce toys and games that encourage the infant to move—to reach, kick, or roll.
- Free infants and toddlers from any unpleasant confinement unless safety is an issue, such as while riding in a car seat. Provide safe spaces and an abundance of time for mobile infants and toddlers to move freely.
- If the toddler seems to be gaining undirected physical momentum, provide a structured opportunity for her to be physically active.
- If the toddler is unable to calm down after physical activity, go to the child individually and, at eye level, calmly invite her to take some deep breaths or do some slow stretches with you. Try moving to slow music and other soothing activities to calm her.

Preschoolers
- During learning-center or outside time, go to the child individually and, at her eye level, suggest activities that may be of interest. Once she shows an interest, begin the activity with her, and then gradually remove yourself, leaving her to continue playing without you.
- During teacher-directed activities, such as story time, add physically engaging activities, such as role-playing or chanting, to draw the child back rather than making commands.
- If the child seems to be gaining undirected physical momentum, provide a structured opportunity for her to be physically active. Let her run or jump in place or move through an obstacle course.
- If the child is unable to engage in an activity after engaging in structured physical release, go to the child individually and, at her eye level, calmly invite her to take some deep breaths with you. Try and transition her into a soothing and relaxing activity, such as water play.

> **Don't** try to make the child be still or maintain eye contact with you. Don't label a child as hyperactive or autistic. These are medical diagnoses that can be determined only by extensive evaluation by medical providers.

Infants and Toddlers
- Healthy infants are active, even before they are mobile. Activity levels will vary among infants.
- After infants become crawlers and walkers, their activity levels increase.
- As with infants, activity levels will vary among toddlers. Toddlers have limited control over their speed and direction as they develop their walking and running skills.
- Five minutes is a long time for a toddler to focus on an activity.

Preschoolers
- Healthy preschoolers are physically active and curious. Activity levels will vary among preschoolers.
- Preschoolers continue to develop and use gross-motor skills, such as running.
- Preschoolers become excited and may momentarily forget rules, such as no running inside.
- Preschoolers learn through discovery and exploration, which requires activity.
- Ten to fifteen minutes is a long time for preschoolers to focus on an activity before becoming fidgety.

PRESCRIPTION FOR PREVENTION

The best solution to hyperactivity is to design spaces, schedules, and curriculum activities to provide many safe opportunities to be active.

Observe
- Recognize which children are becoming antsy and may need to move. Alter their activities to include structured movement. Be flexible when children do not all have to participate or transition at the same time.

Model
- Use appropriate ways of demonstrating physical activity and engagement.

Enhance
- Reduce clutter in the learning environment to avoid visual over-stimulation and use sound-absorbing materials to avoid auditory overstimulation.
- Minimize teacher-directed or structured times and make them optional for children.
- Incorporate gross-motor opportunities into the indoor learning environment.

Language

Observed Behavior

- Raising voice to disturbing level
- Using inappropriate language or words that intimidate other children

Appropriate Response

The immediate priority is to calm and redirect the child while minimizing the effect of the child's shouting or inappropriate language on other children.

Infants and Toddlers
- When an infant makes loud noises or screams, go to him immediately and offer comfort by holding him and talking in soothing tones. Address any physical needs.
- When a toddler is loud, observe him to determine if he seems injured, angry, frustrated, or excited. Immediately address physical injury, following the procedures of the program. For emotional situations, whisper to the child to use a softer voice, acknowledge his feelings, and see if he can show you what caused the outburst so you can help him address the issue.
- When a toddler uses inappropriate language, ignore what he said and redirect him by saying a substitute word that sounds silly or funny. Continue to redirect him to a fun activity.
- If a toddler uses words about toileting frequently and in inappropriate situations, tell him that "we whisper those words" or that "we use those words just in the bathroom."
- If a toddler uses hurtful words, tell him to please stop because hurtful words hurt feelings, and then engage him in another activity.

Preschoolers
- When a preschooler is very loud, observe him to determine if he seems injured, angry, frustrated, or excited. Immediately address physical injury, following the procedures of the program. Ask the child who is loud but not injured to please speak (or groan, and so forth) more softly. Acknowledge his feelings by saying something like, "Casey, you seem upset. Tell me about it." Engage in a conversation, and assist him in resolving the issue.
- If the preschooler frequently raises his voice to a disturbing level after you have addressed his doing so several times, ensure that safety is not an issue and redirect him to a new activity. Encourage other children to continue their activities.
- When a preschooler uses inappropriate language, ignore it. Redirect the child to another activity. If other children call your attention to it, tell them that you heard, but say no more. If the inappropriate language becomes frequent, go to the child and calmly and quietly state something like, "Please do not use that word." Give the child an alternative word to use.
- When a preschooler uses words that intimidate or show lack of respect for other children, place your body between the children involved in the conflict. Assure the

> **Don't** shout back at the child or instruct other children to shout back. Don't emphasize the behavior or shame the child for using words you do not consider appropriate.

child or children who were verbally assaulted that you are there for them. Tell the child who is being offensive to please stop because it is hurtful. Help the children calm down by encouraging them to take deep breaths or hum a song. Facilitate a conversation between the children and then redirect them to activities.

 DEVELOPMENTAL CHECK

Infants and Toddlers
- Infants communicate through their cries, which can become loud.
- Toddlers are continuing to learn about language and may be experimenting with voice level, tones, words, and sounds, such as squeals.
- Toddlers may be learning new words about their genitals and bathroom functions through their toilet training, and they have not learned discretion.

Preschoolers
- Children learn language through imitation. Sometimes preschoolers use language they have heard without understanding its meaning.
- Young preschoolers play with words, including those that may displease adults. They test the sounds and power of words.
- Preschoolers may become excited, fearful, angry, or frustrated and use loud or inappropriate language to express feelings. The child may lack skills to appropriately express feelings.
- Preschoolers may have been successful at getting positive or negative attention from adults when using inappropriate language or screaming; since they feel it works for them, they may continue.

PR_ESCRIPTION FOR PREVENTION

The best solution for children using loud or inappropriate language is to help them develop respect for one another, appropriate ways of expression, and coping strategies. A noisy group of children may indicate active engagement and should not be discouraged.

Observe
- Recognize when children seem to be frustrated, angry, or in the initial stages of conflict with others so you can assist them prior to outbursts.

Model
- Use appropriate ways of verbally communicating with other adults, individual children, and the group. Avoid calling across the room or playground or speaking in unkind tones.

Enhance
- Provide time in the schedule and room in the environment for children to be loud, be it joyful squealing, roaring laughter, giggling, groaning, or other sounds.
- Incorporate relevant materials, such as books about bullying, name-calling, cooperation, and friendship.
- As a substitute for inappropriate language exploration, provide children with vocabulary that has multiple syllables, sounds silly, rhymes, and is from various languages.

Separation Anxiety

Observed Behavior

- Crying and whining by the child when a parent or guardian leaves her in your care
- Reverting to behaviors of a younger child and refusing to participate or interact

Appropriate Response

The immediate priority is to acknowledge the feelings the child is expressing and provide comfort.

Infants and Toddlers

- Hold the infant and provide physical comfort while talking or singing soothingly. Show the infant something visually stimulating, such as bubbles, a mobile, or a toy.
- Reach your arms out and offer to hold the toddler. If she does not want to be held, sit next to her.
- Acknowledge her feelings and say something like, "You look unhappy that your auntie left."
- Reassure her that her family member or guardian will come back and that while she waits she can play.
- Offer a toy that the toddler has shown interest in previously or that a family member or guardian has informed you she likes.

Preschoolers

- Go to the preschooler who is distressed and sit near her. Acknowledge her feelings and invite her to talk about them. Say something like, "You seem pretty upset that your dad had to go to work today. Can you tell me about it?" Let the child know her feelings are okay.
- Ask if a hug or back rub might help her feel better and provide that physical comfort if requested.
- Reassure the child that her family member or guardian will come back. If you know when, show her on the clock or on a picture daily schedule.
- Suggest an activity that the child has shown an interest in previously or that the family member or guardian has informed you she likes. Begin the activity with the child to redirect her.

> **Don't** encourage the family member or guardian to sneak off. Don't take it personally or as a sign that you are not a good teacher. Don't tell the child that big girls and boys do not cry. Don't tell her to stop crying. Don't try to hold the child if she resists physical contact.

DEVELOPMENTAL CHECK

Infants and Toddlers

- Separation anxiety is not an issue for young infants, but it may begin to occur around six months.
- The level of separation anxiety for infants and toddlers will vary and may be influenced by many things, including the child's temperament.
- Older infants and toddlers can be redirected to activities within a few minutes of their family member's or guardian's leaving.
- While toddlers are increasingly interested in independence, they may have times of separation anxiety. They also lack the vocabulary to express their feelings about separation anxiety.

Preschoolers

- Some younger preschoolers may suffer from separation and stranger anxiety, but most have adjusted to separation.
- Older preschoolers who have not experienced separation anxiety for months may feel it renewed when changes occur in their lives, such as family illness, divorce, or a new baby in the family.
- Preschoolers are curious and imaginative, which can sometimes lead to what adults consider unreasonable fears. To the child, however, these fears are very real. New fears may result in the recurrence of separation anxiety.
- Preschoolers continue to develop and use language in more complex ways and are developing a better understanding of time, so a discussion about separation anxiety is possible.

PRₓESCRIPTION FOR PREVENTION

The best solution for separation anxiety is to be prepared for the arrival of the children and warmly welcome each child by name as she arrives. Address any anxiety in a sensitive way.

Observe

- Recognize when individual children experience more separation anxiety so you can be better prepared to assist. Try to determine if the behavior follows patterns, being more likely on certain days of the week, or when the child arrives later or earlier in the day.

Model

- Offer positive greetings, say good-bye cheerfully, use language to express feelings, and become engaged in activities with children.

Enhance

- Encourage family members and guardians to allow enough time for a smooth drop off, so that they are not rushed.
- Provide continuity of care by having consistent teachers. Limit the number of adults to avoid overwhelming children.
- Allow children to bring items from home that may help soothe and comfort them.

Sexualized Behavior

Observed Behavior

- Excessive self-stimulation of genitals
- Comparison of genitals to those of other children or displaying genitals publicly
- Sexual role-playing

Appropriate Response

The immediate priority is to prevent children from touching one another's genitals and to avoid over-reaction to typically developing self-exploration or self-stimulation.

Infants and Toddlers

- When an infant is exploring his genitals or is involved in self-stimulation, ensure that the child does not harm himself, but otherwise allow it. If older children ask about it, explain that the baby is learning about his body.
- When a toddler engages in self-stimulation, check to see if he needs to use the bathroom or is hurting in any way so you can make a medical referral if needed. If there is not a bathroom need or medical concern, then ignore self-stimulation. If it is excessive, redirect the child to an activity that requires his hands.
- When a toddler compares his genitals to another child's, go to the children quickly to prevent them from touching each other and say something like, "Max, you noticed that Jan has a vagina and you have a penis. Please do not touch each other's private body parts." Then help them become interested in an activity that may capture their attention.
- If a toddler has his pants down and is displaying his genitals, calmly investigate to see why. Assist with any physical needs, such as soothing itching insect bites or changing wet clothes. If no health needs are identified, say something like, "Bryson, please pull your pants up. Your penis is a private body part."

Preschoolers

- When a preschooler engages in self-stimulation, ignore it unless the behavior becomes excessive, drawing the attention of others or interfering with the child's routine. If excessive self-stimulation occurs, redirect the child to another activity that requires the use of his hands. In private ask the child if his penis (or her vagina) hurts so you can determine if a referral is needed.
- When a preschooler compares his genitals to another child's, and it appears there may have been physical contact, go to the children and say something like, "Rashid, you noticed that Sarah has a vagina and you have a penis. Boys and girls have some different body parts that are private. Please do not touch each other's private body parts." Answer any questions briefly but honestly. Then help them become interested in an activity that may capture their attention.
- If a preschooler has his pants down and is displaying his genitals, calmly investigate to see why. Assist with any physical

> **Don't** insist that the child stop sexual exploration of himself or self-stimulation unless physical harm is evident.

needs, such as pulling his pants up and moving into the bathroom, soothing itching insect bites, or changing wet clothes. If no health needs are identified, say something like, "Bryson, please pull your pants up. Your penis is a private body part."

 DEVELOPMENTAL CHECK

Infants and Toddlers

- Infants are curious and explore their world first by exploring their own body. Self-stimulation is typical.
- During toilet training, toddlers are focused on the genital area and its function.
- Toddlers recognize that self-stimulation of the genital area feels good and like anything else that feels good to them (thumb sucking, rubbing their favorite blanket, or feeling their mother's hair, for example), they seek it out, especially when they need comfort.
- Toddlers lack modesty and have not yet learned about privacy. Their limited language skills may result in their using their hands to explore things they cannot verbally ask about.

Preschoolers

- Preschoolers are still focused on themselves but have a growing interest in others. They are learning about ways that they are similar and different from each other, including gender differences.
- Typically preschoolers have learned more coping skills than toddlers, but they may still touch their genitals to soothe, comfort, or calm themselves.
- Preschoolers may role-play sexual scenes they have personally experienced, witnessed, or watched on television shows and movies.

PRESCRIPTION FOR PREVENTION

Self-exploration is a natural part of development and should not be prevented. Providing a comforting and nurturing environment that addresses the emotional needs of children may minimize the need for self-stimulation. Close observation and supervision should prevent violent or aggressive sexualized behavior.

Observe
- You can observe to see if children demonstrate sexualized behavior that is not appropriate for their age and make referrals for medical assistance or counseling as needed. If you suspect sexual abuse, it must be reported.

Model
- You can model being comfortable with your own body and sexuality by using correct names for body parts, answering questions briefly but honestly, and remaining calm when children self-stimulate or ask questions about sexuality.

Enhance
- Include activities in the daily curriculum that help teach calming and self-soothing techniques, such as deep breathing, stretching, moving to soft music, water play, and singing.
- Include opportunities in the daily curriculum for children to learn about privacy, modesty, and respect for their own and each other's bodies.
- Use correct terminology for genitals and do not avoid or dismiss questions and concerns children have. See this as one of the many teaching opportunities to help children learn to accept and respect others.

Shyness

Observed Behavior

- Playing alone or near other children most of the time, rarely joining others
- Rarely engaging in meaningful play alone or with other children and demonstrating quiet behaviors of distress, such as rocking or thumb sucking

Appropriate Response

The immediate goal is to comfort a child who may feel rejected and help her build confidence and skills in approaching others to play. It is also important to respect the choice of a child when she prefers to play independently and to recognize cultural differences in interactions.

Infants and Toddlers
- Point out other children and adults to infants and model social behaviors. For example, say something like, "India, look at Bryson. He is playing with his toes. You have toes too. Here they are."
- Limit the number of new people the infant or toddler is exposed to at once, and provide comfort and support if she seems distressed by strangers.
- Go to the toddler who is interested in toys being used by another child and offer a duplicate or alternative toy. Encourage the toddlers to play side by side.
- Go to the toddler who is not welcomed by another toddler or preschooler and acknowledge her feelings of disappointment or anger and redirect her to another activity.
- Encourage toddlers to play short cooperative games, such as rolling a ball back and forth, to give them an introduction to group play.
- Comfort any toddler showing signs of distress and redirect her to an activity of interest.

Preschoolers
- Go to the preschooler who is not welcomed into a group and acknowledge her feelings of disappointment or anger.
- Suggest ways to help the child enter the group. Examples include being helpful, getting toys for the group, playing a role that is not yet claimed, or suggesting ideas.
- If the child is unable to enter the group with your suggestions, offer to play something of interest with the child and encourage her to invite others to join.
- Go to the preschooler who is playing independently and ask if you can play. Try to assess social skills to determine if assistance is needed or independent play is preferred.
- If the child is uninvolved in any activity and is showing signs of distress, try to identify any concerns and reassure her. Then attempt to engage the child in an activity that interests her.

> **Don't** overlook quiet children who do not overtly demand your attention. Don't chastise children for not playing with others or pressure them to interact more. Don't try to require other children to include timid or withdrawn children in their play. Don't label children as shy, timid, or withdrawn, as the reputation may long outlast the behavior.

Infants and Toddlers

- Infants and toddlers tend to be curious about their surroundings, including the people in their environment.
- Older infants and toddlers may experience separation and stranger anxiety.
- Toddlers do not see the point of view of others and cannot share or cooperate well.
- Toddlers use a few words and phrases to communicate but lack the vocabulary to express friendship.
- Toddlers have and show intense feelings, which may be an obstacle to friendship.

Preschoolers

- Younger preschoolers may suffer from separation and stranger anxiety.
- Children whose home language is different from most of the other children's may have more difficulty appropriately expressing their interest in friendship.
- Preschoolers continue to develop and use language in more complex ways.
- Preschoolers lack social skills to always use language appropriately.
- Problem-solving and negotiating skills are being learned and may be practiced.

PR$_x$ESCRIPTION FOR PREVENTION

The best solution for timid and withdrawn children is to provide an environment of acceptance and cooperation.

Observe

- Notice when children seem to be shy or withdrawn. Try to determine if they seem happy playing alone or if they seem to want to play with others but are unable to successfully enter play situations. Determine how to help the child.

Model

- Demonstrate how to enter a group of playing children or how to invite others to play. Use positive language when interacting with others.

Enhance

- Build positive relationships with each child and gently encourage them to practice social and assertive skills with you so you can model and evaluate.
- Actively teach children how to make friends and play together. Plan activities that encourage children to build friendships and work cooperatively, such as class murals.
- Include stories and activities in the daily curriculum that are related to friendship, teams, and courage.

Tantrums

Observed Behavior

- Kicking, swinging arms, throwing things, or whole-body thrashing on the ground or floor
- Screaming or crying during the physical behaviors mentioned above

Appropriate Response

The immediate priority is to keep the child from harming himself or others and to support him in regaining self-control.

Infants and Toddlers
- When an infant uses his body and voice to communicate emotions and needs, his cries should be addressed promptly and warmly.
- When a toddler demonstrates tantrum behaviors, observe from a few feet away, acting busy unless it appears the child is about to inflict immediate harm to himself, others, or property. Assure other children who may inquire about the tantrum that the child will be okay. Tell the other children to continue with what they are doing.
- In the event of potential harm, obtain adult assistance to supervise, reassure, and treat any injuries to other children and to relocate these children if needed. Attempt to remove any object the toddler is using to inflict injury on himself, others, or property.
- After the tantrum has stopped, slowly move physically closer to the child and, as he seems ready to accept it, help him continue to calm down through deep breathing, humming, back rubbing, hugging, cuddling soft toys, or other methods.
- Once the child is calm, help him clean up any mess created by the tantrum, and then help him reenter the group successfully.

Preschoolers
- When a preschooler demonstrates tantrum behaviors, observe from a few feet away, acting busy unless it appears the child is about to inflict immediate harm to himself, others, or property. Assure other children who may inquire about the tantrum that the child will be okay. Tell the other children to continue with what they are doing.
- In the event of potential harm, obtain adult assistance to supervise, reassure, and treat any injuries to other children and to relocate these children if needed. Attempt to remove any object the child is using to inflict injury on himself, others, or property.
- After the tantrum has stopped, slowly move physically closer to the child and, as he seems ready to accept it, help him continue to calm down through deep breathing, humming, back rubbing, hugging, cuddling soft toys, or other methods.

Don't give attention to the child during the tantrum, unless necessary for safety reasons. Don't make fun of the child or call him a baby. Don't try to physically restrain the child unless you have received specialized training or written permission appropriate to your state requirements, and it is necessary for safety reasons.

- Avoid talking about the tantrum, but ask the child how he is feeling. Encourage but do not pressure him to talk about his anger, fear, and other emotions. Validate his feelings, but do not talk about the tantrum behavior. Give him ideas of how to solve the problem that caused the tantrum in case it occurs again.
- Once the child is calm, help him clean up any mess created by the tantrum, and then help him reenter the group successfully.

 DEVELOPMENTAL CHECK

Infants and Toddlers

- Infants do not have tantrums. They use their expressions, bodies, and voices to communicate emotions and needs.
- Toddlers are learning independence and begin to show defiant behavior when things do not go their way.
- Toddlers lack the verbal communication skills to let you know what they want and may resort to tantrums to communicate.
- Toddlers lack self-control and have not yet learned skills to help them cope with their emotions.
- Toddlers imitate adults and other children and may have tantrums if they have seen out-of-control behaviors.

Preschoolers

- Preschoolers are less likely to have tantrums than toddlers. However, younger preschoolers have tantrums at times.
- Preschoolers may have difficulty with a change in routine or daily transitions, and the frustration could escalate into a tantrum.
- Preschoolers are egocentric and see things from their own point of view. Problem solving is therefore limited to the way they perceive a situation. This could cause high levels of frustration, leading to a tantrum.
- As a preschooler's independence increases, it may seem reasonable to the child that they he be able to get or do what he wants, when he wants, and how he wants. When choices are limited, frustration at the lack of control may escalate into a tantrum.

PRESCRIPTION FOR PREVENTION

If you can learn more about why different children have tantrums and what their behavior looks like immediately before a tantrum, you can help the children find alternative ways to express themselves.

Observe

- Notice if children exhibit behaviors that may indicate they have a need they cannot express verbally. Follow up with the child who does exhibit specific behaviors to address the issue before frustration turns into a tantrum.

Model

- Use appropriate ways of verbally expressing your frustration. Model coping and problem-solving skills.

Enhance

- When possible, be flexible with transitions between activities, especially for children who take more time or less time than others.
- Include activities in the daily curriculum that help teach communication, coping, and problem-solving skills.
- Include the opportunity to work off frustration in the daily curriculum through physical activities, such as running, skipping, jumping, dancing, beating a drum, or pounding clay.

Moving Beyond the Crisis

Systematic Observation

Teachers watch children all day long, but can be so busy organizing daily activities that it's often a challenge for them to *really see* each child individually. It's even less likely that they'll see the quiet children who exhibit internalizing behaviors, such as withdrawing from situations, hiding, or failing to engage with others. By observing closely and objectively recording what you see and hear, you can learn a great deal about the children in your group and their behaviors. Observing may help you better understand individual children and begin to see their strengths, interests, family traditions, needs, fears, and other factors that contribute to their personalities and behaviors. Systematic observation helps you see how often a specific behavior really occurs. It may seem as though a behavior occurs frequently, when in reality it happens, for example, only on the playground, just on Tuesdays, when two specific children play together, when you alter the schedule, or many other possibilities. There are many ways to record behavior, including

- anecdotal notes
- running notes
- video recordings
- audio recordings
- checklists
- rating scales
- frequency counts
- time samplings

Give systematic observation a try and see what you can learn about the children you work with. As you begin to notice patterns, it may be possible for you to predict when a challenging behavior is likely to occur, allowing you to take steps to prevent it.

Children Learn from Meaningful and Appropriate Experiences

When working with young children, teaching includes *everything* you do and say. Young children depend on adults to teach them what they need to be successful and happy. You may think that you must focus all of your teaching time on academic activities, such as literacy and math. However, it's critical that you plan for the needs of the whole child and teach social skills, support emotional development, and encourage physical activities. Often the academic skills can be integrated into social-, emotional-, and physical-development areas, but you must not lose sight of the value of addressing a child's total development. Reading a story aloud about an emotional situation integrates literacy with emotional development. Helping children learn appropriate behavior is much like helping them learn any other new skill and requires your planning and support.

Young children do not yet understand the concept of sharing. Keep this in mind when you design the physical space. Include adequate room for play so that children won't be crowded. Try to have several copies of popular toys. Be sure to include materials that encourage self-expression and communication. Provide a daily schedule that is stimulating but not rushed. It should allow for adequate physical activity. Young children should not be expected to sit still for very long. They should be actively involved in fun-filled activities that teach them about getting along in this world. Create a curriculum that is individualized and addresses the strengths, interests, and needs of each child. Help children build their vocabulary so they can use words instead of aggressive behavior. Include conflict resolution, coping, and problem-solving skills in the curriculum. Teach students about friendly and gentle touching, such as shaking hands, patting, and hugging. Help children learn about respect and kindness.

Building Positive Relationships

Building a positive relationship with each child is important and may even help reduce challenging behaviors. To build a positive relationship, it's important to recognize the child's individual interests, needs, temperament, and cultural background. Relationships are not built overnight. They take time and effort. Continuity of care makes such a big difference, and many administrators schedule staff to work with the same children each day. Some programs even arrange for children to stay with the same teacher for years. An adult who is responsible for the care of specific children over a long period of time facilitates close attachment. You are more likely to be supportive and understanding of children with whom you have connected positively. Children are more likely to be cooperative during difficult times if they have a bond with you. A positive relationship tends to make the challenging times go more smoothly for both you and the child.

Respecting Diversity

Some of the families of the children you work with may look and act differently from your own family. Yours may be richer or poorer, larger or smaller. You may have one father instead of two, or a granny rather than a nana. Maybe you were adopted, raised by your aunt, or in foster care. You may have no siblings or a whole bunch. Your family may feel differently about religion, celebrate other holidays, speak another language, and practice "strange" traditions. All of these family characteristics and traditions contributed to who you are now and to what you believe. Although you may not identify with the families of the children you work with, it is important to learn to understand them and demonstrate respect. You want others to respect your family values. You should respect family values that are different from yours.

Welcoming families into the program and establishing a positive relationship from the start is an important strategy for supporting all children. Ongoing communication with families helps build good relationships. Keep families informed of positive daily activities and events. Provide families with information about children's typical development. Inform families of program policies and procedures, as well as of any state or national mandates about discipline. When there is a concern about behavior, avoid alarming families. Instead, help them understand whether or not the challenging behavior is developmentally typical for the child's age. Do not imply that families should punish the child at home for behavior exhibited in your care. If a child's challenging behaviors do not respond to positive guidance techniques and disrupt the learning of the child or others, work in partnership with the family to establish a plan that will support the child's learning of the skills needed for more positive behavior.

Identifying When a Referral Is Needed

Escalating and dangerous behavioral and health concerns may need to be referred to other professionals. Follow your program's procedures. To determine if a referral may be appropriate, conduct systematic observation and document objectively. Be careful to consider children's cultural and linguistic backgrounds and avoid stereotyping or creating bias based on a behavioral incident. Confidentiality must always be strictly respected and care must be taken to provide objective information for referrals only after informed parent consent has been received. If your program does not have funds to pay for such a resource, the referral may simply be a suggestion to parents or guardians to obtain assistance for their child. If there are free or income-based resources in your area, share that contact information with the family.

Working with Other Professionals

Most people agree that two heads are better than one. Other professionals may be able to assist you with providing positive guidance for young children. It can feel lonely and frustrating to go it alone, so seek help and advice for both yourself and the children you care for.

EARLY CHILDHOOD PROFESSIONALS

A peer, supervisor, representative from your local resource and referral agency, or a local college or university instructor may provide possible sources of insight.

- Sometimes having another pair of eyes look at the physical arrangement of the space and provide feedback can be valuable in helping you enhance the learning environment and thus increase positive behavior. Do you have too much open space? Do you have so much furniture that the space is crowded? Are the toys easily accessible, and is it clear where they should be returned to? Do you have sound-absorbing materials to control noise?
- A review of the daily schedule and curriculum activities by another set of eyes may help you see ways to adjust the schedule or add more meaningful experiences for children. Routinely including activities that help children learn skills that may reduce challenging behaviors can be very helpful. Do the children seem pressured and rushed or comfortable and secure? Are the children engaged in the activities and materials provided, or are they moving around aimlessly and bored? Is the sound in the room that of happy exploration or of frustration? Are children using language to express themselves and resolve conflict? Are children using problem-solving skills?

ADMINISTRATORS

Your supervisor, board of directors, or funding source may have resources or the ability to help you network with others to address unmet needs.

- Communicating with your administration about resources needed for supporting positive guidance is essential. On occasion your need may be significant and costly, such as another adult to help ensure the safety of children. But sometimes inexpensive additions can make a world of difference: a secure latch to keep children from opening unsafe spaces; a chime to alert you that someone is entering or leaving; a second play truck to reduce conflict and help children engage in meaningful side-by-side play; a storybook to help a child work through feelings about the new baby at home; puppets to encourage a child to express emotions in safe and acceptable ways. Requesting resources to support positive behavior allows the administrators to plan for and seek needed funds.

HEALTH PROFESSIONALS

A family physician, pediatrician, dentist, audiologist, counselor/psychologist, or other health professional may be able to help identify possible reasons for challenging behaviors and assist with solutions.

- Behavior can sometimes be attributed to health issues. Children may bite because of gum discomfort. A dentist or pediatrician may be more likely to recognize this issue than a teacher. Teachers observing a child consistently scratching her genital area may see it as sexual exploration, but a family physician may see that it could be insect bites in need of treatment. An audiologist may be able to diagnose hearing impairment or ear infection in a child who does not respond to directions or who speaks loudly.
- Counselors may be important resources if challenging behaviors escalate and become dangerous. Professionals bring their perspective and training, helping to expand the assessment of the situation and oftentimes leading to a more comprehensive solution.

Being Ready for Emergencies

In the best of worlds, emergencies may occur as a result of challenging behaviors even when all possible preventive techniques have been exercised. Knowing the steps to take during emergencies will save valuable time when it counts most. Know your program's policies and procedures so that you can react appropriately and quickly. Having a source of communication to summon additional support is critical. Cell phones, intercoms, walkie-talkies, or other such devises should be available at all times.

Taking Care of Yourself

As you work toward learning how to better handle the behavioral challenges you face, remember that taking care of yourself is also important. One way to take care of yourself is through continued professional development. Reading journals, watching DVDs, exploring early childhood Web sites, attending workshops, enrolling in college classes, and finding a mentor will help you become more knowledgeable about typical child development and confident in addressing challenging behaviors. Understanding, supporting, and contributing to your program's policies and procedures will help you know what to do in difficult situations. Asking for resources and help when they are needed shows maturity. It takes a team to deal with difficult issues. Stay well. If you are tired, sick, or burned out, you will have a more difficult time dealing with behavioral challenges. Take a vacation, put your feet up, soak in the tub, and refresh yourself personally and professionally.

Resources for Ongoing Professional Growth

Online Resources

Technical Assistance Center on Social Emotional Intervention for Young Children (TACSEI)

- Funded by the U.S. Department of Education, Office of Special Education Programs, TACSEI has many free online resources, including handouts; training materials; research summaries; "Teaching Tools for Young Children"; a programwide positive behavior support booklet; and more. Check it out.
- 813-974-9803
- www.challengingbehavior.org

Center on the Social and Emotional Foundations for Early Learning (CSEFEL)

- Funded by the Office of Head Start and the Child Care Bureau, CSEFEL has a wealth of free online resources, including training modules; "What Works Briefs," handouts that provide brief research based on information about preventing challenging behaviors; the Book Nook, which provides ideas for using storybooks to support social and emotional development; and "Scripted Stories for Social Situations," which help children understand social skills. Check their Web page for new materials.
- 615-322-3978
- www.vanderbilt.edu/csefel/

Devereux Early Childhood Initiative (DECI)

- DECI offers free online support materials related to social and emotional development and building resilience. Products for sale through Kaplan include the well-known and widely used DECA Kit, a strength-based assessment and planning system to help children develop social and emotional skills. The DECA I/T (Infant and Toddler) Kit and DECA-C (Clinical) Kit are also available. *Facing the Challenge,* a two-part DVD developed in cooperation with Video Active Productions and the National Association for the Education of Young Children, is another instructional tool to help educators better work with children with challenging behavior.
- 610-542-3109 or 866-872-4687
- www.devereux.org/site/PageServer?pagename=deci_index

National Association for the Education of Young Children (NAEYC)

- NAEYC is a professional association that provides free online resources related to many topics including child guidance and discipline. Take a look at their "Early Years Are Learning Years," brief articles designed especially for parents. Their online store features several guidance-related products for sale, including brochures, posters, books, training packs, and the DVD series, *Facing the Challenge.*
- 202-232-8777/800-424-2460 or 866-NAEYC-4U
- www.naeyc.org

ZERO TO THREE: National Center for Infants, Toddlers and Families

- ZERO TO THREE provides free online resources about social and emotional development, temperament, and behavior. Their sections for professionals and parents are both very useful. Products are also available for sale.
- 202-638-1144
- www.zerotothree.org

Resource Books

Caring for the Children, Caring for Yourself: A Guide to Promoting Social and Emotional Health by Judy Whitten, Samantha Hall, Connie Moran, Becky Bennett, and Connie Jo Smith. New York: Kaplan, 2002.

Challenging Behavior in Young Children: Understanding, Preventing, and Responding Effectively by Barbara Kaiser and Judy Sklar Rasminsky. 2nd ed. Boston: Allyn & Bacon, 2007.

A Guide to Discipline by Jeannette Stone. Washington, DC: National Association for the Education of Young Children, 1978.

How Culture Shapes Social-Emotional Development: Implications for Practice in Infant-Family Programs by Rebecca Parlakian. Washington, DC: Zero to Three, 2003.

Meeting the Challenge: Effective Strategies for Challenging Behaviours in Early Childhood Environments by Barbara Kaiser and Judy Sklar Rasminsky. Ottawa, ON: Canadian Child Care Federation, 1999.

Preventing Child Abuse and Neglect: Parent-Provider Partnerships in Child Care by Nancy Seibel, Donna Britt, Linda Groves Gillespie, and Rebecca Parlakian. Washington, DC: Zero to Three, 2006.

The Power of Guidance: Teaching Social-Emotional Skills in Early Childhood Classrooms by Dan Gartrell. Clifton Park, NY: Delmar Learning, 2004.

Week by Week: Plans for Documenting Children's Development by Barbara Ann Nilsen. Clifton Park, NY: Delmar Learning, 2008.

Resources from Redleaf Press
www.redleafpress.org
800-423-8309

Beyond Behavior Management: The Six Life Skills Children Need, second edition by Jenna Bilmes.

Growing, Growing Strong: A Whole Health Curriculum for Young Children by Connie Jo Smith, Charlotte M. Hendricks, and Becky S. Bennett.

Practical Solutions to Practically Every Problem: The Early Childhood Teacher's Manual, revised edition by Steffen Saifer.

So This Is Normal Too? second edition by Deborah Hewitt.

Social and Emotional Development: Connecting Science and Practice in Early Childhood Settings by Dave Riley, Robert R. San Juan, Joan Klinkner, and Ann Ramminger.

Understanding Infant Development by Margaret B. Puckett and Janet K. Black, with Joseph M. Moriarity.

Understanding Preschooler Development by Margaret B. Puckett and Janet K. Black, with Joseph M. Moriarity.

Understanding Toddler Development by Margaret B. Puckett and Janet K. Black, with Joseph M. Moriarity.